LEVEL
3
Fact Reader

Woof!

100 FUN Facts About Dogs

Elizabeth Carney

NATIONAL
GEOGRAPHIC

Washington, D.C.

In memory of Kerry and her unwavering love, loyalty, and comfort. Thank you for being the best dog a girl could have. —E.C.

Copyright © 2017 National Geographic Partners, LLC

Published by National Geographic Partners, LLC, Washington, D.C. 20036. All rights reserved. Reproduction in whole or in part without written permission of the publisher is prohibited.

NATIONAL GEOGRAPHIC and Yellow Border Design are trademarks of the National Geographic Society, used under license.

Designed by Amanda Larsen

Library of Congress Cataloging-in-Publication Data

Names: Carney, Elizabeth, 1981- author. | National Geographic Society (U.S.)
Title: Woof! : 100 fun facts about dogs / Elizabeth Carney.
Other titles: 100 fun facts about dogs | One hundred fun facts about dogs | National Geographic kids.
Description: Washington, DC : National Geographic, [2017] | Series: National geographic kids. Fact readers | Audience: Ages 6-9. | Audience: K to grade 3.
Identifiers: LCCN 2016051363 (print) | LCCN 2017017797 (ebook) | ISBN 9781426329098 (e-book) | ISBN 9781426329074 (pbk. : alk. paper) | ISBN 9781426329081 (hardcover : alk. paper)
Subjects: LCSH: Dogs--Miscellanea--Juvenile literature. | Children's questions and answers.
Classification: LCC SF426.5 (ebook) | LCC SF426.5 .C3745 2017 (print) | DDC 636.7002--dc23
LC record available at https://lccn.loc .gov/2016051363

Photo Credits
GI = Getty Images, SS = Shutterstock
Cover, Gary Randall/Kimball Stock; 1, Purple Collar Pet Photography/GI; 2, Elizabeth Carney; 3, Napat/SS; 4 (UP), Sashkin/SS; 4 (CTR & LO), Eric Isselée/SS; 5 (UP), Chirtsova Natalia/SS; 5 (CTR LE), Matthew Mazzotta; 5 (CTR RT), Ermolaev Alexander/SS; 5 (LO), kali9/GI; 6–7, Alan Jeffery/SS; 8, Holly Kuchera/SS; 9, John Knight/GI; 10, Stefan Cioata/GI; 11 (UP), Photology1971/SS; 11 (LO), Erik Lam/SS; 12, ESB Professional/SS; 13, Sharon Morris/SS; 14, Eric Isselée/SS; 15 (UP RT), alexei_tm/SS; 15 (UP LE), Alzbeta/SS; 15 (LO LE), BoulderPhoto/SS; 15 (LO RT), igorr1/GI; 16, Amanda Nicholls/SS; 17, Susan Schmitz/SS; 18, jasam_io/GI; 19, andresr/GI; 20, LorenzoPatoia/GI; 21, Westend61/GI; 22, Alessandra Sarti/imageBROKER/Alamy Stock Photo; 23 (UP LE), 4kodiak/GI; 23 (UP RT), Jaromir Chalabala/SS; 23 (LO), Tim UR/SS; 24–25, Marcel Jancovic/SS; 26, VitCOM Photo/SS; 27 (UP), Elizabethsalleebauer/GI; 27 (LO), Eric Isselée/SS; 28–29, Spaces Images/GI; 29, Gary Randall/KimballStock; 30, saraidasilva/GI; 31, MisLis/GI; 32–33, Zave Smith/GI; 32 (INSET), Javier Brosch/SS; 34, PM Images/GI; 35, Sebastien Micke/Paris Match via GI; 36 (LE), s5iztok/GI; 36 (RT), Kuttig-People/Alamy Stock Photo; 37, Daniel Grill/GI; 38, Justin Tallis/AFP/GI; 39 (UP), Anton Luhr/imageBROKER/Alamy Stock Photo; 39 (CTR), Pete Oxford/Minden Pictures; 39 (LO), goodluz/SS; 40, Brian Edwards; 41, Jerome Delay/AP Photo; 42, wundervisuals/GI; 43, Humane Society of Missouri; 44 (UP), GI; 44 (CTR LE), REN JF/FEATURECHINA/Newscom; 44 (CTR RT), Eric Isselée/SS; 44 (LO), japape/SS; 45 (UP), Steve Mann/SS; 45 (CTR), dien/SS; 45 (LO), Ermolaev Alexander/SS

National Geographic supports K–12 educators with ELA Common Core Resources. Visit natgeoed.org/commoncore for more information.

Printed in the United States of America
18/WOR/2

Table of Contents

1 Unlike their other canine relatives, African wild dogs have four toes per paw, instead of five.

2 Dogs mostly sweat through glands on their paws.

3 The longest-lived dog on record lived 29 years.

4 Dogs aren't the only animals that bark. Deer, monkeys, and some types of birds also make barking noises.

5 A golden retriever named Augie held five tennis balls in her mouth at one time, setting a world record.

6 The world's fastest dogs—greyhounds—can run about 45 miles an hour.

7 Dogs don't enjoy being hugged. For a dog, putting a limb over another animal is a sign of power and control.

8 Dog poop isn't just gross to step in. A type of parasitic roundworm that can make humans sick is found in more than one-third of dog droppings.

9 Dogs have three eyelids!

25 COOL FACTS ABOUT DOGS

10

Humans have five times the number of taste buds as dogs.

11

Dogs sleep an average of 12 to 14 hours a day.

12

Twelve dogs were aboard the *Titanic*. Three survived—two Pomeranians and a Pekingese.

13

Puppies that have little contact with humans during their first three months usually won't make good pets.

14

From 1924 to 2006, it was illegal to have a pet dog in Reykjavik, Iceland.

15

A park in Cambridge, Massachusetts, U.S.A., has lampposts powered by dog poop.

16

When drinking water, dogs cup the back of their tongues to transfer water from the bowl into their mouths.

17

Poodles get their name from the German word for "to splash dog." They were bred to retrieve birds from lakes and ponds for their hunter owners.

18

A dog belonging to ancient Egyptian royalty got its own tomb near the Pyramids at Giza.

19

Don't be fooled by a hyena's doglike looks. They're actually more closely related to cats.

20

Basset hounds have the longest ears of any breed. They measure between 7 and 10 inches.

21

For a dog, the scent of another dog's poop contains information about that dog's health and mood.

22

The world's tiniest dog is shorter than the length of a toddler's hand.

23

The Chihuahua was named after the state in Mexico where the breed originated.

24

Petting a dog can help you feel relaxed and reduce your blood pressure.

25

Farm dogs in ancient Greece wore spiked collars to protect their necks from wolves as they defended their flocks.

CHAPTER 1

WOLF TO "WOOF"

From Yorkies to bulldogs, ALL DOGS DESCENDED FROM WOLVES.

Dogs are our slobbery, hairy, loyal "best friends." As they lick our faces and drop tennis balls in our laps, it's hard to believe that they used to be wild animals.

Wolves live in family groups, called packs. There can be UP TO 10 WOLVES IN A PACK.

gray wolves

Wolves are fierce hunters. A wolf can eat 20 POUNDS OF MEAT in one sitting.

But if you turned back time thousands of years, scientists believe that you wouldn't find dogs as we know them today. You would find wolves.

Many experts think that thousands of years ago, wolves and humans started to live side by side. The wolves probably ate scraps of food around people's villages. Over time, some animals became tame. They got used to living near humans.

Eventually, these pooches became guard dogs and hunting buddies. They chased away dangerous animals. They ate food that humans threw away. Our friendship with dogs had begun.

Scientists used to think there were three different species of wolves in North America. A new study shows there's only one— GRAY WOLVES.

A wolf's howl can be heard up to 10 MILES AWAY.

Today, there are NEARLY 400 BREEDS OF DOGS. Humans developed them to do all kinds of jobs.

Throughout history, people saw that different breeds had the traits needed to do certain jobs. They bred those dogs together. Over thousands of years, specialized dog breeds came about.

Labrador retrievers have been the MOST POPULAR DOG IN THE UNITED STATES FOR 25 YEARS in a row—the longest streak for any breed.

Labrador retriever

mastiff

Kublai Khan, an ancient Chinese emperor, had 5,000 MASTIFFS. That is believed to be the most dogs ever owned by one person.

Here's an example. In 1989, an Australian breeder wanted a better guide dog for blind people who are allergic to dog hair. Poodles hardly shed. Labradors make good guide dogs. The breeder crossed the two together. The result: Labradoodle puppies!

Labradoodle

CHAPTER 2

DOGS DECODED

Dogs lick people as a SIGN OF AFFECTION.

A dog can make about 100 DIFFERENT FACIAL EXPRESSIONS.

Like their wolf ancestors, dogs are pack animals. They're built to live in family groups and communicate with pack members. TO GET THEIR POINT ACROSS, DOGS BARK, WAG THEIR TAILS, GROWL, YIP, AND HOWL.

How does your dog react when you get home from school? One thing is for sure. Your dog doesn't cry tears of joy. Dogs don't express emotions by shedding tears. Instead, dogs communicate through body language and sound. A happy dog might bark with excitement, give you a lick, and wag its tail—or its whole backside!

A study found that DOGS WERE BETTER ABLE TO FOLLOW HUMAN GESTURES to find hidden food than chimpanzees—our closest animal relatives—were.

Dogs have a wide range of sounds to tell others what's on their mind. Certain sounds usually have certain meanings.

People say beagles and collies are the NOISIEST BREEDS. Akbash and basenji are the quietest breeds.

border collie

BARK: Dogs sometimes make rapid, short barks when they're excited. A slow bark can mean a dog is feeling lonely. Dogs often make loud, quick barks to warn that strangers are coming.

GROWL: Dogs make this low-pitched *grrr* sound when they're angry, fearful, or upset. They'll often hold their ears back and show their teeth. This means "Back off!"

BAY: *Aroooo!* Some dogs make these excited calls when they pick up a scent and are on the chase.

WHINE: High-pitched whines and whimpers often signal that a dog is anxious or in pain. It's the canine way of saying, "I don't feel well."

Tails Tell All!

Dogs don't just say what they're feeling with sound. Body language plays a huge part in how canines communicate. The position of a dog's ears, mouth, and tail tells how it's feeling. A dog's tail in particular is like a billboard that says what it's thinking.

DOGS ONLY WAG THEIR TAILS AT PEOPLE AND OTHER ANIMALS. They don't wag at objects that can't respond.

Wagging back and forth: Means a dog feels relaxed and friendly

Some dogs get so excited that they'll WAG THEIR WHOLE REAR END!

Circling like a pinwheel: Signals a dog feels excited and happy

Angled high: Means a dog feels confident and sure of itself

Standing straight up: Tells you that a dog feels tense, alert, and wary of danger

Tucking down low: Means a dog feels scared and nervous

DOGS CAN FEEL JEALOUS. They act bothered when they see other dogs get treats and they don't.

Wagging low: Tells you that a dog feels worried or uncertain

SOME DOGS don't like being hugged, stroked on the head, or picked up. They view it as threatening.

Most dogs prefer to be petted ON THE CHEST, BACK, OR TUMMY.

It's important to have good canine manners when around dogs. Never try to touch or play with dogs you don't know, unless you have permission. If a dog is showing signs of being nervous, afraid, or angry, leave it alone.

IN DOG LANGUAGE, STARING ISN'T JUST RUDE, IT'S CONSIDERED A THREAT. Don't stare directly into a dog's eyes. If a dog looks tense and is staring at you, move away slowly.

Super Senses

Dogs can sniff out MOLD, INSECTS, DRUGS, and even some CANCERS.

A dog's first sense to develop is TOUCH.

Scientists think dogs can identify smells AT LEAST 10,000 TIMES BETTER than humans can.

Sniff, sniff! Dogs get much more information from a whiff of air than we do. In fact, dogs have both supersniffing and superhearing powers that have been passed down from their ancestors. These powerful senses help them survive.

21

Dogs can DRINK MUDDY WATER and EAT STINKY GARBAGE without getting sick.

Talk about a tough tummy! Dogs have chemicals in their stomachs that kill germs. They can eat things that would normally make people sick. But just because a dog *can* eat garbage doesn't mean it *should*. It can still get sick.

One of a dog's favorite scents is the smell of ROTTING MEAT.

Dogs are carnivores. That means they're built for eating meat, just like their wolf ancestors. But also like wolves, dogs will naturally eat any fruit, vegetable, or grain they can find. Dog food sold in stores contains the grains, meat, fats, and nutrients that keep dogs healthy.

SOME "PEOPLE FOOD" CAN MAKE DOGS SICK. Grapes, raisins, chocolate, and onions—even in small amounts—can be harmful to dogs.

Dogs Up Close

From tail to nose, check out a dog's amazing body.

Dogs' coats vary widely by their breed. Coats can be curly, straight, long, short, coarse, or soft. Some dogs have no coats at all.

A dog's tail is one of its most important methods of communicating. The tail's movement can mean different things.

Strong muscles around dogs' ears allow them to rotate their ears in all directions. This helps dogs pick up sounds more effectively.

It's a myth that dogs are color-blind. They can see colors, just not as vividly as humans do.

A dog has 220 million scent-detecting cells. That's 40 times more than a human has. A dog's nose is usually moist. The wetness helps the dog determine which direction a scent is coming from.

A dog's tongue helps it swallow, taste, groom itself, and regulate its temperature.

CHAPTER 3

DOGS AT HOME AND ON THE JOB

Most puppies will be ready to leave their mothers AFTER 8 TO 12 WEEKS.

Getting a dog is a big commitment. Make sure your family has the space, money, and time needed to care for a dog before bringing one into your home.

There are 77 MILLION pet dogs in the United States alone.

In its new home, a PUP'S HUMAN FAMILY becomes its pack.

MOST POPULAR DOG NAMES

Top Male Dog Names	Top Female Dog Names
Max	Bella
Charlie	Lucy
Buddy	Daisy
Cooper	Lola
Jack	Luna
Rocky	Molly
Bear	Sadie
Duke	Sophie
Toby	Bailey
Tucker	Maggie

Source: American Kennel Club, "These Are the Most Popular Dog Names of 2016"

Puppies

Puppies live off only their mother's milk until they're 4 weeks old. BY 8 WEEKS, THEY'RE EATING ALL SOLID FOOD.

Puppies don't begin WAGGING THEIR TAILS until they're about 6 weeks old.

Large dogs usually have BIGGER LITTERS than small dogs.

A mother dog can give birth to only one pup or as many as 24! ON AVERAGE, DOGS HAVE SIX PUPPIES PER LITTER.

As mammals, newborn puppies drink milk from their mother. Pups are born with a strong sense of smell. But their eyes and the insides of their ears are sealed shut. They depend on Mom for food and warmth.

PUPPIES HAVE 28 BABY TEETH, which fall out when they are 3 to 7 months old. Adult dogs have 42 teeth.

After about 10 days, the pups' eyes and ears open. Soon after, pups have grown enough to start making puppy mischief. They tumble, pounce, and play with their brothers and sisters.

Playtime!

If playtime were a professional sport, puppies would be all-stars. Young dogs have lots of energy. Puppies love activities such as fetching balls, playing with sticks, and chewing toys (and hopefully not furniture!). Play helps pups bond, or form close relationships, with their owners.

Puppies often have a favorite toy.

Most dogs are fully grown by their FIRST BIRTHDAY.

Play helps puppies build skills.

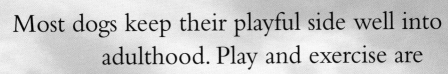

Most dogs keep their playful side well into adulthood. Play and exercise are important for adult dogs to stay happy and fit. Some dogs like to jog with their owners, romp in a dog park, or even go for a swim.

DOGS AGE FASTER than humans do.

Some dogs CAN CATCH A DISK that's been thrown AS FAR AS 400 FEET!

Happy Halloween, Fido! Americans spend about $350 MILLION ON COSTUMES for pets—mostly dogs— each year.

Dog Smarts

Some dogs can learn to FOLLOW COMMANDS BY READING THEM! One dog in New York City raised her paw when she saw the word "wave" and sat when she saw the phrase "sit up."

DOGS ARE CAPABLE OF LEARNING AMAZING TASKS, such as loading a washing machine and getting items out of the refrigerator by name. (But you might be happy if your dog just learned to stop chewing your shoes.)

Dogs didn't become humans' best friend by accident. It helps that dogs are highly intelligent and capable of learning quickly.

Dogs perform many behaviors on cue. Teaching a dog how to follow commands and have good manners is called training. For dog owners, training is very important. Training keeps dogs happy and busy. Dogs enjoy putting their big brains to work.

A border collie named Chaser can IDENTIFY AND RETRIEVE MORE THAN 1,000 TOYS BY NAME.

Training Tips

Good dog trainers understand how dogs learn and what drives them to do what you want. Most dogs are visual learners, or they learn from what they see. They watch humans to see what they want. Combining spoken commands with hand signals can help dogs learn more quickly.

Dogs learn better when training is FUN AND ENJOYABLE.

Most dogs can learn a new behavior IN JUST FOUR TRIES.

You might work for an allowance. But for dogs, food and praise are great rewards for a job well done. When dogs obey a command, offer a small treat and happy-sounding "Good dog!" Never shout at or hit a dog. These methods don't work, and they'll only make a dog afraid.

Dogs on the Job

Humans have worked side by side with dogs for thousands of years. Here are some common dog jobs.

POLICE AND MILITARY DOGS: Some dogs help police officers catch criminals. They can sniff out illegal material.

Most police dogs START THEIR TRAINING between one and one-and-a-half years old.

SEARCH AND RESCUE DOGS: These dogs use their super noses to track a missing person's scent. This can lead rescuers to the person and get him or her to safety.

HERDING DOGS AND GUARD DOGS: These pups help ranchers and farmers keep farm animals safe. They help herd animals from pasture to paddock.

GUIDE DOGS RECEIVE MONTHS OF FORMAL TRAINING before being matched with a partner to serve.

GUIDE AND THERAPY DOGS: Dogs can serve as guide dogs for people who can't see. They can do tasks for people who are sick or disabled. Some dogs bring comfort to people in the hospital.

Working dogs often have the following traits: a desire to bond with people, INTELLIGENCE, MOTIVATION by food or toys, and an ABILITY TO FOCUS.

Piper, a border collie in Traverse City, Michigan, U.S.A., CHASES BIRDS FROM THE RUNWAY, helping to make takeoff and landing safer for planes.

Piper isn't the only pooch with an unusual job. In Virunga National Park in central Africa, bloodhounds use their nose to track illegal hunters. This helps keep wildlife, like endangered mountain gorillas, safe.

Dogs have been TRAINED TO HUNT down the scat, or poop, of many types of animals. Examples include Iberian wolves, tigers, spotted owls, and cougars.

In Seattle, Washington, U.S.A., scientists team up with dogs to collect data on animals. These "conservation canines" sniff out an animal's poop. Then a scientist scoops up the samples for study. The samples can tell the scientist about the health and number of that kind of animal in the area.

Many dog owners heard about their pooches from family members or people they know. ABOUT A QUARTER OF OWNERS ADOPTED THEIR DOGS FROM A SHELTER OR ANIMAL RESCUE CENTER.

SOME ANIMAL SHELTERS HAVE PROGRAMS FOR KIDS TO READ TO DOGS. This helps dogs become less nervous around humans.

Scientists have found that owning a dog is related to health benefits for humans, too. These include reduced stress, better heart health, and a higher level of physical activity.

One company creates CUSTOM DOGHOUSES that are designed to look like owners' homes. The most expensive models cost $35,000!

For many dogs, the most important job of all is bringing love and joy to their family.

1

A dog's whiskers can sense tiny changes in airflow.

2

SONY, a Japanese electronics company, made a robotic dog called AIBO, the Japanese word for "companion."

3

At age one, a dog has the same level of physical development as a 15-year-old human.

4

When a sleeping dog twitches and moves its paws, it's probably dreaming.

5

A dog can smell half a teaspoon of sugar in an Olympic-size pool.

6

The most expensive dog in the world—a Tibetan mastiff—was bought in China for $1.9 million.

7

Dogs can smell your feelings. Chemicals in your sweat change when you become nervous or fearful, and dogs can detect that.

8

In 2014, the prestigious Westminster dog show allowed mutts to compete for the first time—in the agility competition.

9

After doing their business, some dogs kick the ground backward to further mark their territory.

10

The Norwegian lundehund sports six toes on each foot.

25 MORE FACTS ABOUT DOGS

11

Depending on their breed, dogs can sprint 19 miles an hour.

12

The sound of a human yawning can trigger a yawn in a dog.

13

The average dog's intelligence is about at the level of a two-and-a-half-year-old human.

14

Newfoundlands have webbed paws, which help them swim better.

15

Dogs have around 18 muscles to control the movement of their ears. No wonder a dog's ears are so expressive.

16

A seeing-eye dog once helped his blind owner hike all 2,100 miles of the Appalachian Trail.

17

Prairie dogs aren't dogs at all. They're members of the squirrel family.

18

Basenjis are the only dog breed that can yodel.

19

Some scientists think the first dogs were tamed in central Asia, around modern-day Nepal or Mongolia.

20

Most dogs' tongues are pink. But some breeds, like chows and shar-peis, have black tongues.

21

Dogs pant to cool themselves.

22

Dogs have better night vision than humans.

23

Extreme fear of dogs is called cynophobia.

24

Dogs' taste buds can detect five flavors—sweet, sour, bitter, fruity, and umami (meaty).

25

A dog's nose print is as unique as a human fingerprint.

DOG FACTS ROUNDUP

WOOF!
You've been trained in the doggy details. Did you catch all 100 facts?

1. Unlike their other canine relatives, African wild dogs have four toes per paw, instead of five. 2. Dogs mostly sweat through glands on their paws. 3. The longest-lived dog on record lived 29 years. 4. Dogs aren't the only animals that bark. Deer, monkeys, and some types of birds also make barking noises. 5. A golden retriever named Augie held five tennis balls in her mouth at one time, setting a world record. 6. The world's fastest dogs— greyhounds—can run about 45 miles an hour. 7. Dogs don't enjoy being hugged. For a dog, putting a limb over another animal is a sign of power and control. 8. Dog poop isn't just gross to step in. A type of parasitic roundworm that can make humans sick is found in more than one-third of dog droppings. 9. Dogs have three eyelids! 10. Humans have five times the number of taste buds as dogs. 11. Dogs can sleep an average of 12 to 14 hours a day. 12. Twelve dogs were aboard the *Titanic*. Three survived—two Pomeranians and a Pekingese. 13. Puppies that have little contact with humans during their first three months usually won't make good pets. 14. From 1924 to 2006, it was illegal to have a pet dog in Reykjavik, Iceland. 15. A park in Cambridge, Massachusetts, U.S.A., has lampposts powered by dog poop. 16. When drinking water, dogs cup the back of their tongues to transfer water from the bowl into their mouths. 17. Poodles get their name from the German word for "to splash dog." They were bred to retrieve birds from lakes and ponds for their hunter owners. 18. A dog belonging to ancient Egyptian royalty got its own tomb near the Pyramids at Giza. 19. Don't be fooled by a hyena's doglike looks. They're actually more closely related to cats. 20. Basset hounds have the longest ears of any breed. They measure between 7 and 10 inches. 21. For a dog, the scent of another dog's poop contains information about that dog's health and mood. 22. The world's tiniest dog is shorter than the length of a toddler's hand. 23. The Chihuahua was named after the state in Mexico where the breed originated. 24. Petting a dog can help you feel relaxed and reduce your blood pressure. 25. Farm dogs in ancient Greece wore spiked collars to protect their necks from wolves as they defended their flocks. 26. From Yorkies to bulldogs, all dogs descended from wolves. 27. Wolves live in family groups, called packs. There can be up to 10 wolves in a pack. 28. Wolves are fierce hunters. A wolf can eat 20 pounds of meat in one sitting. 29. Scientists used to think there were three different species of wolves in North America. A new study shows there's only one—gray wolves. 30. A wolf's howl can be heard up to 10 miles away. 31. Today, there are nearly 400 breeds of dogs. Humans developed them to do all kinds of jobs. 32. Labrador retrievers have been the most popular dog in the United States for 25 years in a row—the longest streak for any breed. 33. Kublai Khan, an ancient Chinese emperor, had 5,000 mastiffs. That is believed to be the most dogs ever owned by one person. 34. Dogs lick people as a sign of affection. 35. A dog can make about 100 different facial expressions. 36. Like their wolf ancestors, dogs are pack animals. They're built to live in family groups and communicate with pack members. To get their point across, dogs bark, wag their tails, growl, yip, and howl. 37. A study found that dogs were better able to follow human gestures to find hidden food than chimpanzees—our closest animal relatives—were. 38. People say that beagles and collies are the noisiest breeds. Akbash and basenji are the quietest breeds. 39. Dogs only wag their tails at people and other animals. They don't wag at objects that can't respond. 40. Some dogs get so excited that they'll wag their whole rear end! 41. Dogs can feel jealous. They act bothered when they see other dogs get treats and they don't. 42. Most dogs prefer to be petted on the chest, back, or tummy. 43. Some dogs don't like being hugged, stroked on the head,

or picked up. They view it as threatening. 44. In dog language, staring isn't just rude, it's considered a threat. Don't stare directly into a dog's eyes. If a dog looks tense and is staring at you, move away slowly. 45. Dogs can sniff out mold, insects, drugs, and even some cancers. 46. A dog's first sense to develop is touch. 47. Scientists think dogs can identify smells at least 10,000 times better than humans can. 48. Dogs can drink muddy water and eat stinky garbage without getting sick. 49. One of a dog's favorite scents is the smell of rotting meat. 50. Some "people food" can make dogs sick. Grapes, raisins, chocolate, and onions—even in small amounts—can be harmful to dogs. 51. Most puppies are ready to leave their mothers after 8 to 12 weeks. 52. In its new home, a pup's human family becomes its pack. 53. There are 77 million pet dogs in the United States alone. 54. Puppies live off only their mother's milk until they're 4 weeks old. By 8 weeks, they're eating all solid food. 55. Puppies don't begin wagging their tails until they're about 6 weeks old. 56. A mother dog can give birth to only one pup or as many as 24! On average, dogs have six puppies per litter. 57. Large dogs usually have bigger litters than small dogs. 58. Puppies have 28 baby teeth, which fall out when they are 3 to 7 months old. Adult dogs have 42 teeth. 59. Most dogs are fully grown by their first birthday. 60. Dogs age faster than humans do. 61. Some dogs can catch a disk that's been thrown as far as 400 feet. 62. Happy Halloween, Fido! Americans spend about $350 million on costumes for pets—mostly dogs—each year. 63. Some dogs can learn to follow commands by reading them! One dog in New York City raised her paw when she saw the word "wave" and sat when she saw the phrase "sit up." 64. Dogs are capable of learning amazing tasks, such as loading a washing machine and getting items out of the refrigerator by name. 65. A border collie named Chaser can identify and retrieve over 1,000 toys by name. 66. Dogs learn better when training is fun and enjoyable. 67. Most dogs can learn a new behavior in just four tries. 68. Most police dogs start their training between one and one-and-a-half-years old. 69. Guide dogs receive months of training before being matched with a partner to serve. 70. Working dogs often have the following traits: a desire to bond with people, intelligence, motivation by food or toys, and an ability to focus. 71. Piper, a border collie in Traverse City, Michigan, U.S.A., chases birds from the runway, helping to make takeoff and landing safer for planes. 72. Dogs have been trained to hunt down the scat, or poop, of many types of animals. 73. Many dog owners heard about their pooches from family members or people they know. About a quarter of owners adopted their dogs from a shelter or animal rescue center. 74. Some animal shelters have programs for kids to read to dogs. This helps dogs become less nervous around humans. 75. One company creates custom doghouses that are designed to look like their owners' homes. The most expensive models cost $35,000! 76. A dog's whiskers can sense tiny changes in airflow. 77. SONY, a Japanese electronics company, made a robotic dog called AIBO, the Japanese word for "companion." 78. At age one, a dog has the same level of physical development as a 15-year-old human. 79. When a sleeping dog twitches and moves its paws, it's probably dreaming. 80. A dog can smell half a teaspoon of sugar in an Olympic-size pool. 81. The most expensive dog in the world—a Tibetan mastiff—was bought in China for $1.9 million. 82. Dogs can smell your feelings. Chemicals in your sweat change when you become nervous or fearful, and dogs can detect that. 83. In 2014, the prestigious Westminster dog show allowed mutts to compete for the first time—in the agility competition. 84. After doing their business, some dogs kick the ground backward to further mark their territory. 85. The Norwegian lundehund sports six toes on each foot. 86. Depending on their breed, dogs can sprint 19 miles an hour. 87. The sound of a human yawning can trigger a yawn in a dog. 88. The average dog's intelligence is about at the level of a two-and-a-half-year-old human. 89. Newfoundlands have webbed paws, which help them swim better. 90. Dogs have around 18 muscles to control the movement of their ears. No wonder a dog's ears are so expressive. 91. A seeing-eye dog once helped his blind owner hike all 2,100 miles of the Appalachian Trail. 92. Prairie dogs aren't dogs at all. They're members of the squirrel family. 93. Basenjis are the only dog breed that can yodel. 94. Some scientists think that the first dogs were tamed in central Asia, around modern-day Nepal or Mongolia. 95. Most dogs' tongues are pink. But some breeds, like chows and shar-peis, have black tongues. 96. Dogs pant to cool themselves. 97. Dogs have better night vision than humans. 98. Extreme fear of dogs is called cynophobia. 99. Dogs' taste buds can detect five flavors—sweet, sour, bitter, fruity, and umami (meaty). 100. A dog's nose print is as unique as a human fingerprint.

INDEX

Boldface indicates illustrations.